SLOATSBURG PUBLIC LIBRARY
J 975.3 San   SLOL
Sandak, Cass R.
The White House /

3 2849 00262 6879

D1793108

J
975.3
S

Sandak, Cass R.
The White House

DATE DUE			

SLOATSBURG PUBLIC LIBRARY
SLOATSBURG, NEW YORK 10974

THE WHITE HOUSE

THE WHITE HOUSE

BY CASS R. SANDAK

Franklin Watts
New York/London/Toronto/Sydney/1981
A First Book

To Letitia Baldrige

Cover photograph courtesy of: Fred J. Maroon/Photo Researchers, Inc.

Photos courtesy of:
Frontis: Conklin from Monkmeyer Press Photo Service;
p. viii: Washington Convention and Visitors Bureau;
p. 3: Franklin D. Roosevelt Library;
p. 8: Library of Congress;
pp. 11, 15, and 16: New York Public Library Picture Collection;
p. 20: White House Historical Association;
pp. 23, 29, 32, 35, 38, and 41: United Press International, Inc.;
p. 46: Rutherford B. Hayes Library;
p. 50: United Press International, Inc.;
p. 57: United Press International, Inc.

Library of Congress Cataloging in Publication Data

Sandak, Cass R
The White House.

(A First book)
Bibliography: p.
Includes index.
SUMMARY: Presents a historical sketch of the White House, describes the interior and exterior of the mansion, and portrays life in the White House.
1. Washington, D.C. White House—Juvenile literature.
2. Presidents—United States—Juvenile literature.
[1. Washington, D.C. White House. 2. Presidents]
I. Title.

F204.W5S26   975.3   80-25350
ISBN 0-531-04254-5

Copyright © 1981 Cass R. Sandak
All rights reserved
Printed in the United States of America
6 5 4 3 2

CONTENTS

Introduction
1

A Brief Historical Sketch
4

*The White House Enters
the Twentieth Century*
12

*The White House
Inside and Out*
19

Life at the White House
42

Conclusion
56

For Further Reading
59

Index
60

THE WHITE HOUSE

Fountains play on the South Lawn of the White House. The President and his guests often use the ground-level entrance under the South Portico.

INTRODUCTION

Sixteen hundred Pennsylvania Avenue is the most famous address in America, and one of the most distinguished in the world. This is the White House, in Washington, D.C., where the President of the United States lives and works.

Apart from the Capitol, where our laws are made, the White House is probably the most important building in the United States. Within its walls, decisions are made that may affect the lives of all Americans and have worldwide significance.

The White House is constantly in the news. Newspapers, magazines, radio and television broadcasting networks from all over the world maintain large staffs of reporters in Washington. Some are assigned only to cover news from the White House. Almost every day there is something to report—an important meeting, a speech, a news conference, or an awards ceremony. Since we hear so much about the White House, it is important to know more about the place where the President and the First Family live.

Every President since John Adams has lived in the White House. Even George Washington, the only President who never lived there, helped to choose the site and approve the design for the building. The White House was the first public building erected when the new capital city of Washington was planned in the late eighteenth century. But in a sense, the White House is also the last to be completed. Because each presidential family makes changes and brings something individual to it, the work on the White House is never truly finished.

From the beginning, the White House has been a symbol of American pride. The building is nearly as old as the country itself. Tracing its history leads us through almost two hundred years of our nation's growth, and touches upon the lives of all of our national leaders. The furnishings of the White House —the antiques and mementos of the past—are important because of what they tell us about the people who used them. These are the souvenirs of America's great men, and they have the power to stir our pride and fire our imagination.

The White House is a showcase of American history. President John F. Kennedy once said in an interview that having "Grant's table, Lincoln's bed, Monroe's gold set . . . makes these men more alive . . . makes the White House a stronger panorama of our great story." The history of the White House is the story of the people who lived there.

There President Lincoln signed the Emancipation Proclamation, and President Franklin D. Roosevelt announced the declaration of war with Japan and drew the nation together with his fireside chats. In speeches televised from the White House, President Lyndon B. Johnson outlined his program to build the "Great Society," and Lady Bird Johnson launched her campaign to beautify the capital city as well as the nation. From there President Richard M. Nixon ended the conflict in Vietnam and resigned the office of the Presidency. And from the White House, President Jimmy Carter often addressed the country regarding the economic situation, the energy crisis, and developments abroad.

Visitors come not just to see the beautiful house and its grounds, but also to learn more about the Presidents and their families, and—at the same time—more about the American experience. In addition to the wealth of furnishings and other possessions of former Presidents, the White House displays a unique and almost complete collection of portraits of the Presidents and their wives.

*During his presidency,
Franklin D. Roosevelt often broadcast
fireside chats to the nation from the White House.*

In the United States, many of the homes built by the wealthy are larger and grander than the White House. However, the White House is the true seat of power. But even though the President is a very powerful man—the leader of the greatest country on earth—he is still responsible to the American people who elect him to office. And as a reflection of this democratic ideal, the White House—in addition to being the private home of the President while he is in office—is also a public home, a home that belongs to the entire nation.

A BRIEF HISTORICAL SKETCH

Washington and the White House Are Planned

The White House is situated in the heart of Washington, D.C. It was the first major public building undertaken in the new "Federal City," the site chosen to succeed New York and Philadelphia as the nation's permanent capital. In these cities President Washington and his wife Martha had lived in a number of different houses. When the White House was begun, the city of Washington was still a wilderness of marshlands and dense woods. The only buildings were pigsties and shacks.

Major Pierre L'Enfant, a French-born engineer and architect, was appointed to lay out the new city of Washington by President Washington himself. First he chose a magnificent site for the Capitol building, on a hill near the center of his plan for the city. To the northwest of this spot, he selected the site for the President's House.

Even before they had a plan for the building, Major L'Enfant and President Washington agreed upon the requirements for the President's House: it should have "the sumptuousness of a palace, the convenience of a house, and the agreeableness of a country seat." In 1791, President Washington approved the site selected by L'Enfant for the house—a rise of land just north of the Tiber Creek, which marked the southern boundary of the White House grounds until the 1880s, when it was filled in.

From the Capitol, L'Enfant planned the major avenues of the city to extend outward, crossing other streets to form a grid designed for future development. He planned Washington's major avenue to run from Rock Creek, through the site selected for the President's House, past the foot of Jenkins Hill, now Capitol Hill, to end at the Anacostia, a small river in the southeastern part of the city. This path is now Pennsylvania Avenue, the most famous parade route in the country. The distance between the Capitol building and the White House is about one and a half miles.

To make Washington's and L'Enfant's dreams a reality, the Congress of the infant nation set aside $200,000 from the meager national treasury to construct the house. This was a generous sum of money in 1792, and a handsome home was anticipated.

In 1792, the Commissioners of the District of Columbia sponsored a contest for the best design for the President's House. James Hoban, an Irish-born architect practicing in Charleston, South Carolina, won the design competition and the $500 prize.

Hoban's design called for a house with a long, low, rectangular shape. His design was based on the work of Palladio, the most influential architect of the Italian Renaissance. Hoban used popular design books and builders' guides. He apparently picked up ideas for his design from two European palaces that had been built earlier in the eighteenth century. The north facade of the White House looks very much like the palace of the Duke of Leinster in Dublin, Ireland. The south side strongly resembles the garden facade of the Château de Rastignac in France.

Thomas Jefferson did not like Hoban's plan. For one thing, he thought the house was "big enough for two emperors, one Pope, and the Grand Lama." After Jefferson became President, however, he asked architect Benjamin Latrobe to add the terraces, or pavilions, on the east and west sides. Among the columns of the ground level arcades, service and storage rooms for wine, ice, meat, poultry, horses, and quarters for servants were ingeniously hidden.

Construction on the White House began in 1792. Contrary to many popular stories, President Washington was not present when the ground was broken and the cornerstone laid on October 13, 1792. George and Martha Washington were at that time living in the city of Philadelphia, the temporary capital of the country. Building continued slowly for eight years, as money and workers were in short supply. In 1797, John Adams became President, and Washington withdrew from public life to his Mount Vernon estate in Virginia. Unfortunately, he died before he could see the President's House completed.

John Adams Moves In

Only six rooms were finished when John Adams, our second President, moved into the President's House during his last year of office. The house was first occupied on November 1, 1800. The next day, in a letter to his wife Abigail, who joined him later, President Adams wrote: "I pray heaven to bestow the best of blessings on this house and all that shall hereafter inhabit it. May none but honest and wise men ever rule under this roof." Adams's words were a prayer not only for the White House, but for the entire nation. In 1940, President Franklin D. Roosevelt had these words inscribed on the mantel over the fireplace in the State Dining Room. On leaving the still unfinished White House at the end of President Adams's term of office, Mrs. Adams wisely predicted that this would be a house for ages to come.

The White House Is Burned

On August 24, 1814, British soldiers burned the White House during the attack on Washington in which they also set fire to the Capitol building. But first, soldiers marched right into the President's dining room and helped themselves to food which the hastily departing servants had left on the table. Dolley Madison herself, President James Madison's wife, had heroically stayed behind in the house until the very last minute, trying to save as many valued belongings as possible. She managed to fill a wagon with important papers relating to the early history of the United States. We owe to Dolley Madison's efforts also the full-length portrait of George Washington painted by Gilbert Stuart which now hangs in the East Room. Even though the British could be seen advancing, she refused to flee from the house until the picture had been broken out of its frame and entrusted to friends.

Fortunately, a violent rainstorm that night quenched the flames of the fire and thus two of our greatest national treasures —the Capitol building and the White House—were saved from total devastation. Of the White House, only the smoke-blackened outer walls and the interior brickwork remained standing.

In 1814, the British burned the White House. Only the outer walls of the building remained standing.

The White House Is Rebuilt

In 1815, architect James Hoban was called in to rebuild the White House according to his original plans. To cover the stains caused by smoke and fire, the light gray sandstone walls were painted white. However, there is evidence that white paint had been used before the fire, and that the President's House had been called the White House even earlier. In 1811, Francis James Jackson, the British Minister in Washington, had referred to the building as the White House, because the light sandstone walls looked white in contrast to the dark red brick of the city's other homes and buildings. A newspaper had used the term White House in 1813. It was not until 1902, however, that President Theodore Roosevelt made the name White House official and had his stationery imprinted with it.

James Monroe and his wife were the first presidential family to occupy the newly rebuilt White House in 1817. Their experiences as American representatives at Napoleon's court had introduced them to French manners and taste. This was reflected in the French Empire furnishings they chose. The Monroes introduced a formal elegance and style to the decoration and entertainment at the White House.

For a time, Benjamin Latrobe served as the official White House architect, but it was Hoban who built the South Portico in 1824 and the North Portico in 1829. The designs for the porticos are a combination of Hoban's and Latrobe's ideas. These additions completed the basic construction on the building.

Plans to Build a New White House

In the mid-nineteenth century, some Presidents felt that the White House should be replaced. They thought the house was too small. And, just to the east and south of the grounds, an unhealthy waterway called the City Canal had been built. It ran into the center of a noisy and dirty market area. Malarial mosquitoes bred in the canal. In the hot summer months, many of the Presidents fled with their families to cool and comfortable estates in nearby Maryland and Virginia, just as more recent Presidents have retreated to Camp David to rest and relax away from the city and the Oval Office.

The City Canal was compared to a great open sewer. About 1870, army engineers drained and cleaned this area. Responsibility for the maintenance and improvement of the White House was under the Army Corps of Engineers from 1869 to 1925. The National Park Service assumed these responsibilities in 1925, and today they are still in charge of the grounds.

At various times during the 1800s, some members of Congress proposed that the White House should be relocated to a healthier place, away from the dirt and dust of the city and the unhealthy Potomac marshes. Nothing ever came of these plans.

Tired of being crowded in the second-floor living quarters, several Presidents and their wives asked architects in the late nineteenth century to draw up plans for expanding the living and office spaces at the White House. Mrs. Benjamin Harrison came up with the grandest scheme.

With only one bathroom for her large family—Mrs. Harrison's aged father, a married son and daughter and their spouses, and three grandchildren—it is easy to see why Mrs. Harrison complained about the lack of space. She proposed adding huge wings to the House that would dwarf the original central block. Her plans included an enormous greenhouse that would extend nearly a thousand feet across one side of the new building. Fortunately, Congress did not take Mrs. Harrison's plans seriously. Today, Mrs. Harrison is remembered chiefly as the founder of the White House china collection. A few years later, President William McKinley proposed another outrageous

This old print shows Ulysses S. Grant's children being driven to school from the White House.

architectural plan that called for huge domed pavilions to be built. These plans as well were never developed.

No major structural changes were made to the White House between the completion of the North Portico in 1829 and the Roosevelt renovations of 1902, with the exception of the greenhouses that President James Buchanan had constructed on the West Terrace. Other Presidents added more greenhouses in the late nineteenth century.

In 1873, President Grant ordered several rooms to be renovated because of sagging ceilings and rotting timbers. Following these reconstructions, several rooms were decorated in the ornate style of the period.

With each administration and each new presidential family, the White House decor moved further away from Hoban's original designs. When Chester Alan Arthur became President in 1881, he refused to move into the White House until he had the entire mansion refurnished to his taste. The new decor included exotic plants and a stained glass screen designed by Louis C. Tiffany. To make room for his plush furnishings, President Arthur had twenty-four wagonloads of furniture and other bric-a-brac sold at public auction.

THE WHITE HOUSE ENTERS THE TWENTIETH CENTURY

In 1902, when President Theodore Roosevelt and his family moved into the White House, they found a chaotic mixture of decorating styles. They also found the living quarters on the second floor too cramped for their large family. Congress therefore appropriated half a million turn-of-the-century dollars for restoration efforts. The Roosevelts removed the huge greenhouse from the West Terrace, enlarged the State Dining Room, and rebuilt much of the interior, reinforcing walls and floors. They succeeded in bringing back a restrained elegance to the White House and its historic rooms.

President Roosevelt also moved the presidential offices out of the main living quarters and into the newly constructed West Wing. This office building was planned as only a temporary addition, but it was further expanded and remodeled in 1909, and again in 1927 and 1934. An entrance and colonnade were also added at the East End in 1902. The East Wing offices, built in 1942, have become the center for the First Lady's activities.

In 1927, President Calvin Coolidge had the attic reconstructed to create more living space. A sunroom was constructed over the South Portico. Here the family gathered to relax, and Mrs. Coolidge did her sewing and attended to her personal correspondence.

The added weight of the fireproof materials used in the reconstruction of the attic considerably weakened the already strained walls of the White House. Cracks in the plaster of the rooms and hallways below began to show, and even further damage was revealed when the walls were later reconstructed during President Harry S. Truman's restoration. In 1929, a fire caused some damage to the West Wing, but it was soon repaired.

In the 1930s, Franklin D. Roosevelt had the first modern kitchen installed on the ground floor. An indoor swimming pool was built in the West Terrace for FDR, after the White House physician stressed the President's need for regular exercise. Because the President had been stricken with poliomyelitis as a young man and was confined to a wheelchair, swimming was thought to be the best form of exercise, since the water could support him while his unsteady legs could not. Funds for the President's pool came from contributions from all over the country.

During his first term of office, President Truman added the balcony behind the columns of the South Portico at the second-story level. When it was built in 1948, the Truman balcony stirred much debate around the country. People thought the balcony would destroy the beauty and dignity of the house, but the balcony has stayed and has been popular with presidential families ever since.

The Truman Restoration

Toward the end of his first term in the White House, President Truman became alarmed by the poor condition of the structure. While working in his study late one evening, he felt the whole room swaying. At night, when the house was quiet, mysterious cracking and creaking noises would be heard. On another occasion, a piano leg crashed through a section of decayed flooring. In 1948, Truman called in a team of architects and engineers to examine the White House thoroughly. The investigating committee concluded that the White House was an unsafe firetrap standing "purely from habit." The building was ready to collapse.

Some experts recommended that a new White House could be built for less money than the needed repairs would cost. But national sentiment prevailed. The White House that had witnessed more than a century and a half of our nation's history was well worth saving—even at great expense. Congress therefore approved a budget of 5.4 million dollars for the much needed reconstruction and modernization.

The reconstruction took almost four years. Workmen com-

Above and over: between 1948 and 1952, the White House was completely rebuilt, both outside and inside. Years of wear and tear had made the building unsound.

pletely dismantled the White House, except for the outer walls. Bricks, nails, and even bits of lumber from the original house were sold as souvenirs. Workers tried to use as much of the original material as possible in reconstructing the house with strong, durable, fireproof materials. In their work, they found many signs of the building's history—charred timbers from the 1814 fire and the names of workmen who originally built the White House.

The historic state rooms were reproduced almost exactly, and many new rooms were added. Foundations were dug two stories deep in the ground and the whole basement structure was reinforced with thousands of cubic yards of concrete. A steel framework was erected inside the walls. Two new basement levels provided additional room for storage and utility areas. A television broadcasting room was created on the ground floor level. Special ducts in the walls and ceilings concealed pipes, wires, and heating lines. A central air-conditioning and humidity control system was installed throughout the house, as well as an internal telephone system and a synchronized electric clock system. Under the East Wing, a well-equipped bomb shelter, large enough for the First Family and some of the White House staff, was constructed.

While the construction work proceeded, President Truman and his wife and daughter lived for more than three years across Pennsylvania Avenue at Blair House, a stately brick town house that is used as a guest house for official presidential visitors.

In 1952, when the Trumans moved back into the completely renovated White House, they were told that the house should last another five hundred years! The total cost of repairs was approximately 5.8 million dollars. Today, such extensive restoration work would cost many times this amount.

The Trumans hoped the interior could be furnished with

antiques and historic pieces. But funds were short and in many cases they had to settle for reproductions of historic furnishings. After the Trumans, the Eisenhowers occupied the renovated White House. They maintained the traditional decor established by their predecessors.

The Kennedys and the White House Historical Association

Mrs. John F. Kennedy wanted the White House furnishings to be more authentic and to reflect our nation's history, as well as American traditions of craftsmanship. Her ideas did have a precedent. In the 1920s, Grace Coolidge asked Congress to pass legislation allowing the White House to accept gifts of appropriate antiques. Later, the Herbert Hoovers assembled the historic pieces now in the Lincoln Bedroom. Mrs. Kennedy formed the Fine Arts Committee to restore the White House. They decided that an early nineteenth-century style was most appropriate for many of the public rooms. The Committee hoped to make a number of the rooms look much as they might have when the Monroes moved into the house in 1817. They sought donors to replace reproductions of period furnishings with original antiques, and they looked for funds to continue restoration work over the years to come.

The Fine Arts Committee was successful in bringing to light many original White House furnishings that had been in dusty storerooms for decades. Many other valuable pieces were found in private collections around the country. In 1961, Mrs. Kennedy was instrumental in forming the White House Historical Association, which initiated an ambitious program of books and publications concerning all aspects of the White House and its contents. Finally, she focused national attention on the restoration work being undertaken there with her televised tour of the White House that was seen by more than eighty million viewers.

Thanks to Mrs. Kennedy's efforts, Americans began to take a renewed patriotic pride and interest in the White House. The first curator of the White House collections was hired by Mrs. Kennedy. Later, in 1964, President Johnson created the Committee for the Preservation of the White House and established the permanent post of White House Curator. The work of the White House Historical Association has continued under Lady Bird Johnson, Pat Nixon, Betty Ford, and Rosalynn Carter.

THE WHITE HOUSE INSIDE AND OUT

A View of the White House

The main section of the White House is shaped like a box 168 feet (51.20 m) long, 85 feet 6 inches wide (27.40 m), and 70 feet (21.33 m) high at the highest point. Until 1902, this was all there was to the White House, except for the low, broad terraces and the large greenhouses which have since been torn down. The White House is larger than most people's homes, but it is still much smaller than the palaces of many foreign leaders, and smaller than many homes built by the wealthy in our own country.

On the north and south sides of this great block are the two porticos which help to give the White House its distinctive appearance. The North Portico, with its twelve Ionic columns, was completed by Andrew Jackson. It looks out upon Pennsylvania Avenue and Lafayette Square, where a statue of Jackson was erected in 1853. Under the North Portico is the main entrance.

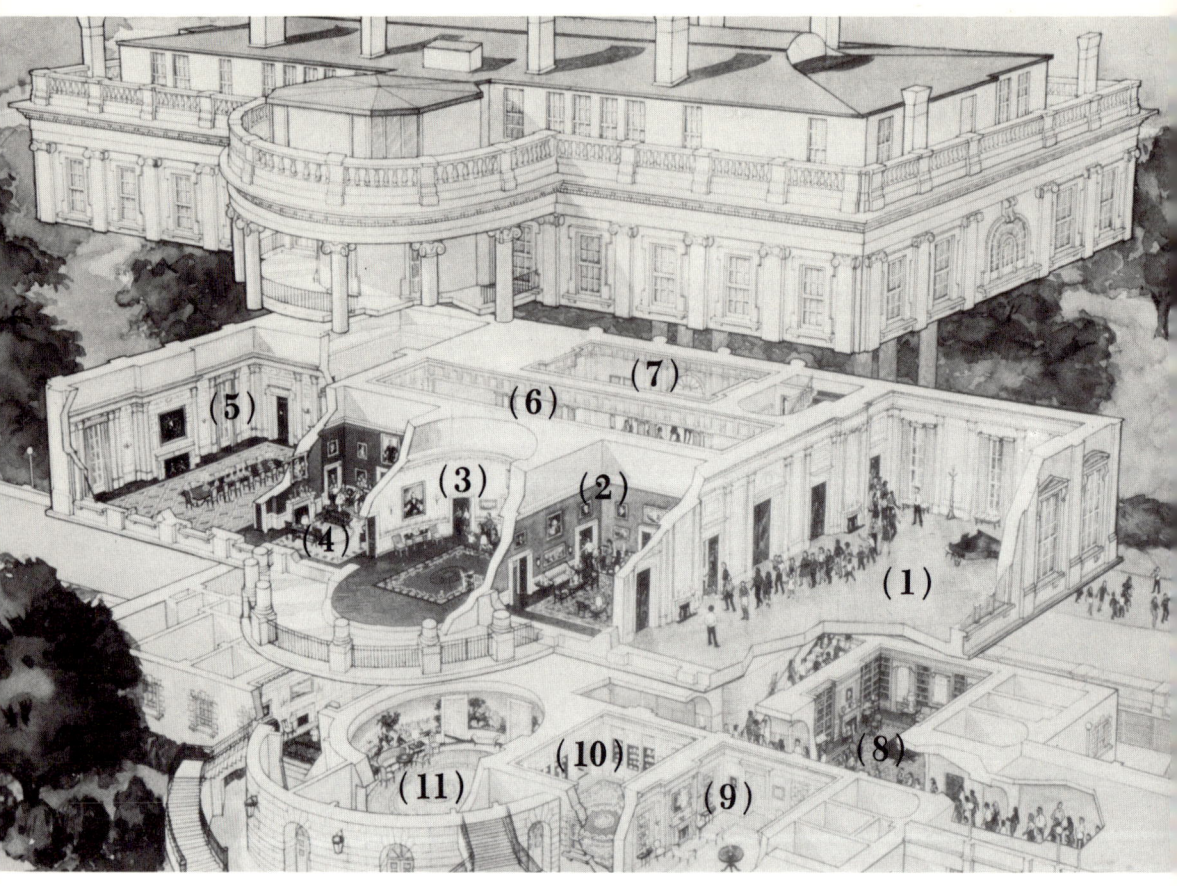

(1) East Room
(2) Green Room
(3) Blue Room
(4) Red Room
(5) State Dining Room
(6) Cross Hall
(7) Entrance Hall
(8) Library
(9) Vermeil Room
(10) China Room
(11) Diplomatic Reception Room

A cutaway view of the White House showing some of the most famous rooms.

From this side, only two stories of the White House are visible. The balustrade, or railing, that runs along the edge of the building above the second story hides the third or attic story tucked under the hipped roof.

Only from the sloping lawns on the south side of the house can the windows of the ground floor of the White House be seen. This side of the house is dominated by the South Portico. It is curved to follow the swelling contour of the south side of the house where three tiers of oval-shaped rooms are located. A representation of the South Portico is on the back of the twenty-dollar bill.

From the east and west sides of the main section of the White House, low galleries extend out to the office wings. These galleries serve as corridors to the East and West Wings. The roofs of these galleries provide pleasant terraces. The West Terrace has frequently been used for outdoor receptions and dinners.

The Oval Office

When we think of the White House as a private residence, it is easy to forget that it is also the place where decisions are made that can affect all our lives. For more than one hundred years, the President's working offices were crowded in with the First Family's cramped living quarters on the second floor. Swarms of sightseers, lobbyists, and people seeking presidential favors crammed the halls, stairways, and landings. Before the West Wing offices were built in 1902, anyone who wanted to see the President just walked into the White House and climbed the stairs to the President's offices on the second floor. The British author Charles Dickens was appalled when he visited the White House in 1842 and saw men lounging around in chairs, waiting to see the President and spitting tobacco juice on the carpets at the same time.

Today, the three-story West Wing flanks the West Terrace. The West Wing is where the President and his staff do most of their work. Only official visitors who have important business with the President are allowed here. President Nixon made the most recent changes to the West Wing in 1969, when he added a driveway and a small portico on the Pennsylvania Avenue side. He altered the room where official visitors wait before being ushered in to see the President. Before press conferences, newspaper and television reporters wait in another room constructed in the West Terrace where the FDR pool had been.

When the President is ready to receive a visitor, the guest is led into the President's oval-shaped office. Usually, the President will rise from his chair to greet visitors. He shakes their hands and tries to make them feel at home. Often, he stands in front of the great carved desk, which some of the Presidents have used. Only Kennedy and Carter have used this desk in the Oval Office itself. Britain's Queen Victoria gave the desk as a special gift to the American people in 1880.

On the right side of the presidential desk stands a United States flag; to the left is the President's flag. The Presidential Seal, based on the Great Seal of the United States, is molded into the ceiling plaster. In cool weather, a fire may blaze in the marble fireplace on one side of the room. Sometimes the President sits chatting with guests in armchairs placed in front of the fire.

Glass doors open from the President's office onto a small covered porch and lead into the Rose Garden beyond. In good weather, the President often meets with guests and representatives from foreign countries in this garden. Sometimes he holds press conferences here or pins awards and decorations on men

A 1980 conference in the Rose Garden between President Carter and Anwar Sadat, Egypt's President.

and women who have served the country in special ways. President Kennedy honored our first men in space at ceremonies held in the White House Rose Garden.

In the West Wing are offices for the Vice President, the Secretary of State, and the Chief of Staff. The Cabinet Room is also located here. Thomas Jefferson coined the term Cabinet when George Washington surrounded himself with a circle of top level advisers, thus creating the first Cabinet posts. Today, in addition to the Cabinet members, the President's staff consists of about 600 employees. Other presidential staff members include the more than 1,200 members of the Secret Service and the 800 members of the Executive Protective Service. Recent Presidents have also employed "detailees" from the armed forces and from other government agencies for temporary duty on various assignments directly under the President's control.

Obviously, all of these people cannot possibly work right in the White House. Next to the White House, at the junction of Seventeenth Street and Pennsylvania Avenue, stands the Old Executive Office Building. Built between 1871 and 1888, it is one of the most impressive office buildings in Washington. The exterior is like a wedding cake of carved white marble. Inside are suites of plush, comfortable offices with high ceilings and ornate hallways. Several of the White House aides involved in the Watergate scandal had offices in this building. A new, smaller Executive Office Building has been constructed across Pennsylvania Avenue near Blair House.

The First Lady's Office

The First Lady and her staff have offices on the second floor of the East Wing. It is linked to the main building of the White

House by the East Terrace. The East Wing was begun in 1902 during Theodore Roosevelt's renovations. In 1942, it was rebuilt and expanded. Underneath the East Wing, the first White House bomb shelter was constructed, and at the same time a tunnel was dug leading to the Treasury Building. Although this tunnel is no longer open, rumor has it that at least one White House bride used it to escape eager crowds following her wedding reception.

Visitors who come to see the First Lady often wait in a wood-paneled lounge. Or guests may choose to wait in the sunny, less formal Garden Room that overlooks the Jacqueline B. Kennedy Garden, an area of green lawn lined with trees and beds of bright flowers. Sometimes the First Lady likes to meet her guests in the garden.

Entering the White House

When the President and First Lady invite high-ranking guests to attend an important official function, the guests of honor come into the White House through the North Entrance under the North Portico. Guests used to arrive here in horsedrawn coaches and carriages. Foreign dignitaries and heads of state still use this entrance when they come to the White House for a state dinner or luncheon.

Guards check the identities of all other guests as they enter the grounds through the southwest gates. Most guests invited to the White House go in through the ground level Diplomatic Reception Room on the south side. Members of the First Family may also use this South Entrance when they come home from school or a romp in the garden, or when they leave for an important trip or public appearance. Other, less distinguished guests sometimes use another entrance on the side facing Pennsylvania Avenue. It is located at the far end of the East Terrace. The main public entrance—where tourists enter—is on the east side of the East Wing.

The Ground Floor

Directly inside the South Entrance is the oval-shaped Diplomatic Reception Room. Originally, this room was an ugly cellar space filled with boilers and hot water pipes. Now it is an elegant room decorated in an early nineteenth-century style. The antique wallpaper is handprinted with scenes of American natural beauty—places like Niagara Falls and Natural Bridge in Virginia. Jacqueline Kennedy acquired this rare and beautiful paper from a house that was about to be torn down. The paper was carefully removed and then fitted to the walls of the Diplomatic Reception Room during Mrs. Kennedy's extensive renovation of the house. This was the room that President Roosevelt had used for broadcasting his famous "fireside chats" to the American people during the late 1930s.

Also on the ground floor are a number of other interesting rooms. They are connected by a vaulted corridor that serves as a gallery for portraits of many of the First Ladies. The intimate Library has a select collection of books and furnishings. Space for more books is located upstairs in the First Family's private living quarters. On the walls of the Library hang portraits of native Indian chiefs by the American painter Charles Bird King.

Few visitors get to see the other ground level rooms. The main kitchens for the White House have always been located on this floor. The China Room and the Vermeil Room are two special rooms set aside to display porcelain, silver, and giltware pieces that are among the White House's most prized possessions. A map room holds a fine collection of maps, prints, and charts. A physicians' office and a well-equipped clinic are located on this floor. Finally, two other offices occupy the ground floor level, including an office for the White House Curator, who works with the First Lady in caring for and improving the collection of furnishings, presidential mementos, and works of art.

A Visit to the White House

Among the homes of world leaders, the White House is unique in being open to the public. Every morning except Sundays, Mondays, and holidays, the principal rooms may be seen between ten and twelve noon. Today, the White House welcomes nearly two million public and official visitors each year. But all except the President's close personal friends and important guests are restricted to a tour of the state rooms of the house.

Public visitors to the White House state rooms enter through the door in the East Wing and pass through the East Wing corridor on the ground floor level. The windows in this corridor command a fine view of the Jacqueline B. Kennedy Garden and the grounds to the south. Displays show the story of the White House—furnishings, family, and social history.

The State Rooms

The five state rooms on the first floor of the White House are the best-known and best-preserved part of the house. These are the rooms where important ceremonial functions involving the President take place. A tour of these rooms begins with the East Room and extends through the Green, Blue, and Red Rooms, passes through the State Dining Room on the west side of the house, and ends in the front Entrance Hall.

The East Room

After climbing a marble staircase, visitors find themselves outside the magnificent East Room, the largest room in the entire White House. It is 80 feet (24.38 m) long and 37 feet 2 inches (11.54 m) wide. It has functioned as the grand reception hall and ballroom ever since the room was completed some twenty-nine years after the rest of the house was occupied. Gold draperies and crystal chandeliers hang in the room where Abigail Adams once hung her family wash. Elegant furniture lines the walls. The parquet floor has no carpet, but the housekeeping staff keeps it shiny and bright.

Because the East Room is so large, it has been put to many uses. During the Civil War, Union soldiers were quartered here. The bodies of seven of the eight presidents who died in office lay in state in the East Room while thousands of mourners filed past. After her husband's assassination in 1963, Jacqueline Kennedy had the black draperies that hung in the East Room at President Lincoln's funeral copied from an old print. The actual funeral services of five of our Presidents—William Henry Harrison, Taylor, Lincoln, Harding, and Franklin D. Roosevelt—have been held in the East Room.

But the room has also seen laughter and merriment. Theodore Roosevelt's children used to roller-skate over the polished floors of the sparsely furnished room. In 1906, President Roosevelt's daughter "Princess Alice" married Congressman Nicholas Longworth in this same room. Some sixty years later, Lynda Bird Johnson chose the same site for her wedding in 1967. At this event, Alice Roosevelt Longworth was one of the honored guests.

The East Room is where guests usually gather before state dinners. The room is often used for parties and receptions and can accommodate a large number of guests. In one part of the

Many official functions and receptions are held in the spacious grandeur of the famous East Room.

room is a grand piano decorated with scenes of American folk dance and musical life. The gilded legs of the piano are in the shape of eagles. There is a story that Grace Coolidge dared to play a few chords on the East Room piano (an earlier one) when she visited the White House as a young schoolteacher. Of course, at the time she never dreamed that later she would live in the White House and be First Lady.

    The White House has a tradition of inviting distinguished artists to perform. Famous singers, dancers, and musicians have appeared at the White House before the President and his guests. A portable stage can be assembled in the East Room. When President Millard Fillmore invited Jenny Lind, the "Swedish nightingale" of the 1850s, the East Room was too small to accommodate all the people who wanted to hear her sing. Therefore, Miss Lind sang on the White House lawn in front of thousands of delighted guests.

The Green, Blue, and Red Rooms

We have little idea of how the inside of the White House looked before the British burned it in 1814. The Monroes were the first presidential family to occupy the rebuilt White House in 1817. Many of their decorating ideas and some of their furnishings have remained with us—especially in the three parlors known as the Green, Blue, and Red Rooms.

The Green Room

James and Elizabeth Monroe first decorated the Green Room with green draperies and upholstery. Jacqueline Kennedy and Pat Nixon chose a similar green decor during their 1962 and 1971 refurbishments.

    Our early Presidents used the Green Room for different

purposes. Thomas Jefferson made it his private dining room. Madison used it as a sitting room, and Monroe used it as a card room where gentlemen gathered to smoke and play cards after dinner parties. John Quincy Adams made the Green Room a quiet drawing room, and it has remained so ever since.

Today, the Green Room has been refurnished with fine early nineteenth-century American furniture. Even though the pieces are more than one hundred and fifty years old, they look brand new! Over the fireplace in the Green Room hangs a famous portrait of Benjamin Franklin wearing his invention—bifocal spectacles.

The Blue Room

The Green Room opens into the oval-shaped Blue Room. James Hoban, the original White House architect, planned the Blue Room to be the focal point of the whole house. Of the three oval rooms—including the Diplomatic Reception Room below and the Yellow Oval Room above—it is the best-known. The original color scheme of the room was red, but the Martin Van Burens first used blue in the room, and blue it has remained.

Three huge windows look out over the beautifully landscaped gardens. Until 1824, when the South Portico was completed, the French doors of the Blue Room served as the south entrance to the White House. In President Monroe's time, the room was lighted by fifty candles set in a gilded chandelier. Monroe ordered elegant gilded furniture from Paris, and some of the same furniture is still used today in this room.

The Blue Room is about 40 feet (12 m) long and 30 feet (9 m) wide. The President often uses the Blue Room for his receiving line when large numbers of guests come. Receptions and afternoon teas for hundreds of guests can be held in the Blue Room.

One of three oval-shaped rooms, the Blue Room is shown after the 1963 restoration to the decor of President Monroe's time.

The Red Room

The walls of the Red Room are covered with red satin. Around the edges, the red walls have a gold border. The same red and gold design is repeated in the Red Room's sofas and chairs. The Red Room was first used by the family of John Adams as a breakfast room, and by Thomas Jefferson as a sitting room. Dolley Madison made the room her Yellow Drawing Room. On Wednesday evenings, she opened the room up for her glittering "at-homes," when hundreds of callers were welcomed. Now a portrait of Dolley Madison, one of Washington's all-time favorite hostesses, gives life to the same room where she held her lively gatherings.

The James Polks first established the red decor in the 1840s. In 1962, Jacqueline Kennedy restored the Red Room to an early nineteenth-century style. In the nineteenth century, the Red Room was used by many First Families as a parlor for big Sunday evening gatherings of aunts, uncles, and cousins.

In 1877, the most significant event in the room's history took place. The presidential race that year between Samuel J. Tilden and Rutherford B. Hayes had failed to produce a clear winner with a majority of votes. Hayes was selected by a specially appointed electoral committee. He was sworn in as President late on a Sunday evening in a secret ceremony held in this room. Two days later, the official inauguration ceremony of President Hayes was held at the Capitol.

The State Dining Room

The State Dining Room in Hoban's original plans was much smaller than the room we see today. By 1850 it was clear that it was far too small to seat all the important guests who were expected to attend the state dinners given for government officials and foreign diplomats. By removing a wide stairway in the hall next to the room, the dining room was almost doubled in size during Theodore Roosevelt's 1902 renovation. The room can now seat 140 dinner guests. Decorating the table is a 13 foot (4 m) long centerpiece with mirrors and gilded figures. This centerpiece was among the furnishings ordered from France by President Monroe. Over the marble mantelpiece is the famous seated portrait of Abraham Lincoln.

Opposite the State Dining Room is the smaller and less formal Family Dining Room. This room is generally not seen by the public on a visit to the White House. The Family Dining Room is used for smaller dinner parties given by the President and members of his family. Sometimes, the President hosts informal breakfast and luncheon meetings here for friends and members of his Cabinet and staff. Usually, however, the President and his family eat most of their meals upstairs in a much smaller private dining room in their living quarters.

The Entrance Hall

At the end of the tour of the first floor state rooms, visitors to the White House find themselves in the impressive Entrance Hall. This is where state visitors enter and get their first impressions of the White House. The vista from the Entrance Hall is awe-inspiring. Looking south, one can see through the windows of the Blue Room the white marble dome of the Jefferson Memorial framed by expanses of trees and lawn. Slightly to the left is the majestic Washington Monument. The Entrance Hall opens into the Cross Hall, around which the state rooms are grouped. This marks the end of the public tour of the White House. Only official guests and friends of the President and his family are allowed to see the other parts of the house.

President Lincoln looks down from above the fireplace, while President Gerald R. Ford (at right) and other leaders enjoy dinner in the State Dining Room.

The Second Floor

On the second floor is the Yellow Oval Room, which was an office for some presidents before the West Wing was constructed in 1902. In 1850, Mrs. Millard Fillmore established the first White House library in this room. Now it is used as a formal drawing room. Flanking a broad doorway in the room are two flags. These are used in the special ceremony that takes place before state dinners and other official functions. The flags in the Yellow Oval Room are removed from their places by a two-person color guard and are carried out the door and down the grand staircase. The President and the First Lady and state visitors then follow down the steps to the first-floor Entrance Hall, as members of the Marine Band dressed in colorful scarlet uniforms play "Hail to the Chief," traditionally the President's official song. The Marine Band continues to play as the parade of guests moves through the Entrance Hall and into the State Dining Room where formal dinners take place.

Next to the Yellow Oval Room is the former Presidential Cabinet Room, now called the Treaty Room. In this room, in 1902, President Theodore Roosevelt signed the treaty that ended the Spanish-American War. Important meetings still take place here.

The second and third floors of the White House are now off limits to the public, because the President and his family live there. Until 1902, when President Theodore Roosevelt reconstructed the second floor and added the Executive Offices in the West Wing, the family living quarters were very cramped. Legend says that when they first moved in, on one occasion, four of President Roosevelt's six children slept crosswise on a bed in the Lincoln Bedroom. The bedroom where the President and First Lady sleep is in the southwest corner of the second floor. A suite of rooms used by Amy Carter is on the Pennsylvania Avenue side, behind the North Portico.

The Lincoln Bedroom

The Lincoln Bedroom was once the Cabinet Room, where President Lincoln signed the Emancipation Proclamation in 1863, outlawing slavery in the United States. Now the Lincoln Bedroom and the Lincoln Sitting Room next to it form a suite for male guests of honor who stay at the White House. Great Britain's King George VI and Prince Philip both stayed in this room at different times.

Most of the objects in the room are associated with President Lincoln and it is easy for those who visit the room to feel the great man's presence. Some people say that it is as if the spirit of President Lincoln had never departed from this place. Other people claim that the room is actually haunted by Lincoln's ghost! Two weeks before his assassination, President Lincoln dreamed of his own death and saw his casket placed in the black-draped East Room below. Lincoln believed in omens and told several people about the dream. He was a somewhat mystical man, and Mrs. Lincoln often invited spiritualists to hold seances in the White House.

The Queens' Bedroom

Across the hallway from the Lincoln Bedroom is the Rose Bedroom or Queens' Bedroom. Five reigning queens, as well as other distinguished guests, have stayed in this room. Former Queen Juliana of the Netherlands was the first guest to stay in the bright and friendly room after the Trumans moved back into the White House in 1952. One of the most treasured gifts in the White House is the mirror that Princess Elizabeth of Great Britain presented to the United States in 1951, a year before she became queen. The eighteenth-century mirror was presented to the White House with inspiring words about the deep affection and cultural ties between the people of Britain and America.

Lyndon B. Johnson escorts members of the press through the Lincoln Bedroom in 1963.

The Third Floor and Roof

Storage rooms, guest rooms, and some additional living space are located on the third floor. In the third story, or attic, of the White House, hidden behind the curved balustrade above the South Portico, is the solarium. The President's family uses this as an extra living room. Informal parties and get-togethers are often held here. Some Presidents have relaxed by preparing simple meals for their friends in the kitchenette that opens off this sunroom. During President Kennedy's term of office, the sunroom was used as a classroom for Caroline Kennedy and other children who were instructed here by special tutors.

Even the White House roof has its stories. All through World War II, military personnel armed with powerful machine guns were stationed on the White House roof to protect the house against any attack. Earlier still, President Grant's son Jesse who had a passion for astronomy, set up his telescopes on the roof. And President Lyndon B. Johnson often held Texas-style cookouts here on a terrace outside the solarium.

The White House Grounds

The White House stands on 18 acres (7.20 hectares) of carefully landscaped grounds surrounded by a high iron fence. Guards protect the gates which serve as entrances to the grounds. Circular driveways curve around the front and back of the house. The English boxwood hedge near the main entrance under the North Portico on Pennsylvania Avenue was planted in 1870. Near the tennis courts is a garden designed just for children. It includes an apple tree and a goldfish pond.

Close to the house are semiformal terraces and gardens. The first White House gardens were planned for President and Mrs. Adams, but we have little idea what they were like. In 1851, Andrew Jackson Downing made the first comprehensive plans for the White House grounds. The famous Rose Garden is located just outside the President's office in the West Wing. President Nixon's daughter Tricia was married in the Rose Garden.

In 1970, President and Mrs. Nixon started a new tradition by opening up the White House gardens to the public on one Saturday and one Sunday afternoon each spring and fall. Each year, thousands of visitors from all over the country and all over the world line up outside the East Gate for the annual garden tour. Guides lead groups of people through the gardens. Markers showing pictures of past Presidents and events which took place in that location are set up to point out things of interest: an oak tree planted by President Eisenhower or a magnolia from President Jackson's plantation. Jackson planted the magnolias in memory of his beloved wife Rachel, who died before Jackson moved into the White House.

The south side of the White House grounds is a private park for the President and his family. This area of wooded groves, flower beds, and broad lawns is open to the public only during the spring and fall garden tours and on Easter Monday. On that day, children gather for the annual Easter Egg Roll on the lawn. Adults are allowed to come only if they are accompanied by a child!

Dolley Madison, wife of President James Madison, started the annual Easter Egg Roll for the children of Washington. At first, the event was held on the grounds of the Capitol. But Lucy Hayes, the wife of President Rutherford B. Hayes, brought the happy custom to the White House lawn, where the Easter Egg Roll has been held ever since.

When the President uses a helicopter, small red squares marking the landing area are set into the turf of the South Lawn. Other heads of state coming by helicopter land on the

An aerial view of the White House and grounds from the north. Offices are located in the East and West Wings that flank the main building.

Ellipse, an area south of the White House grounds. They are then taken by limousine to the White House to meet the President and to receive a twenty-one gun salute.

LIFE AT THE WHITE HOUSE

Everyone who has ever lived or worked in the White House has left something of his or her own personality behind and thus added a new page to the continuing story of the building. The character of life at the White House is a blend of formality and informality based upon the demands of official life and the personal life-styles of the people who lived there. Thomas Jefferson's informal personal philosophy let him answer the door himself and receive his guests padding about the rooms in his bedroom slippers. However, under Jefferson, elegance also became a White House tradition. At his frequent and popular dinner parties, he introduced many new foods he had become acquainted with abroad, including ice cream and macaroni.

Some stories about the household arrangements at the White House seem refreshingly democratic. We smile as we imagine Abigail Adams hanging the family wash to dry in the unfinished East Room and then presiding at an evening party for distinguished visitors. President William Henry Harrison took a wicker basket to the nearby open-air markets to do his own grocery shopping. Today these scenes of an earlier, simpler life seem very remote. Now a Chief Usher is appointed to supervise the large White House staff of household employees. It is his or her duty to call the plumber if one is needed, and to keep careful accounts of all White House expenditures.

Continuing Improvements and Increasing Comforts

Advances in many fields of science and technology have been reflected in the rising standard of living in American homes. Throughout the nineteenth and twentieth centuries, America's houses have grown increasingly more comfortable, efficient, and well-equipped, and the story of technological improvements at the White House reflects this pattern.

When the Adamses moved into the White House in 1800, there was no well on the premises. Servants had to carry buckets of fresh, cool water from a spring a mile and a half away. A few years later, Thomas Jefferson had a cistern built in the attic to collect rainwater. Gravity carried the water through wooden pipes to the kitchen and to other rooms in the stories below. President Van Buren had water storage tanks installed in the White House basement. A system of pumps was used to carry water to the kitchen and bathrooms.

Around 1833, the first pipes carrying running water through all parts of the house were installed, but a fully equipped bathroom was not built in the White House until the 1880s. This bathroom, with its heavy porcelain fixtures, was similar to our modern bathrooms, but for many years there was only one. After getting stuck in an old White House bathtub, President William Howard Taft had a special tub built for himself large enough for his huge body. An old photograph shows four workmen sitting in it!

The first central heating system in the White House was a hot air furnace installed in 1845. President Franklin Pierce had a hot water furnace installed in 1853, and President Polk had gas lighting fixtures put in in 1849. In 1879, Thomas Edison invented the electric light bulb, and the White House was one of the first homes in the country to be wired for electricity. In 1891, President Benjamin Harrison had electric wires run throughout the White House. Edison also gave the President one of the earliest models of his other new invention—the phonograph.

In 1877, President Hayes asked Alexander Graham Bell personally to install his new invention, the telephone, in his office. In their first conversation over the new instrument, President Hayes spoke into the receiver on his desk to Bell over 13 miles (20.92 km) of newly installed telephone wires.

The first White House elevator was built in 1881 and was run mechanically. Today there are five electric elevators in the White House and its wings.

President Taft was the first President to use an automobile while in office. He maintained a fleet of four classic cars. President Warren Harding was the first President to ride to his inauguration in an automobile. In 1921, Harding listened to a broadcast over the first White House radio.

The list goes on and on. The Presidents and their families were among the first to use many of the brilliant American inventions: the typewriter, the sewing machine, the refrigerator, television. But sometimes this willingness to embrace the new carried its own burden of problems. Workers cutting through floors, walls, and ceilings to install the profusion of pipes, wires, and other systems the White House had never been designed to hold seriously weakened the structure. This is one of the reasons the White House came so near collapsing during the Truman administration.

First Ladies and the White House

Today, the presidential apartments in the White House consist of thirty rooms, sixteen bathrooms, one kitchen, two elevators, and a solarium. The White House—excluding the office wings—has 132 rooms. In addition, the White House has many of the facilities of a modern town, including a barber shop, a movie theater, and a bowling alley. A swimming pool is located on the grounds behind the West Wing. There is also a well-equipped gymnasium for the President and his staff members. Obviously, running such a large establishment requires great skill and energy.

Just as the President is responsible for running the country, the First Lady is responsible for running the White House. The story of life at the White House is largely the story of the First Ladies who have lived there. The personalities of the First Ladies have been directly reflected in their styles of entertainment at the White House. Angelica Van Buren offended the entire country with her supposed extravagance. She had become fond of European customs during her visits to the courts and capitals of Europe and introduced foreign foods and manners when she served as First Lady for her father-in-law. Lucy Hayes was known as "Lemonade Lucy" because she refused to serve any drink stronger than lemonade at White House parties and receptions.

The best-loved First Ladies have been warm, outgoing, and energetic. Julia Dent Grant is remembered as one of the happiest First Ladies, delighted with her family and life at the White House. Edith Roosevelt was famous for the skill and ease with which she controlled her large, rambunctious family and ran the White House, as some said, without ever making a mistake! For exercise, Edith Wilson, President Wilson's second wife, rode a bicycle through the White House corridors. During her husband's long illness, it is said that she ran the country!

Not all the First Ladies have been Presidents' wives. Because Thomas Jefferson's wife Martha had died nineteen years

Mrs. Lucy Hayes and two of her children in one of the White House greenhouses.

before he became President, Mrs. Thomas M. Randolph and Mrs. John Wayles Eppes, Jefferson's daughters, acted as official hostesses at White House functions. In addition, Jefferson was frequently assisted by Dolley Madison, a young lady whom he introduced to Washington society in 1801. Other presidents have been widowers or bachelors, while others had wives who were too ill to perform the many duties required of them.

The Housekeeping Staff

In general, the First Lady supervises the White House housekeeping staff through her housekeeper. The White House employs a housekeeping staff of almost one hundred people. Money is appropriated annually by Congress to maintain the house and its grounds in good order. Permanent staff members include engineers, maintenance people, gardeners, butlers, ushers, doormen, cooks, maids, and chauffeurs. A storekeeper oversees marketing and household supplies. A messenger runs urgent errands, and the housekeeper supervises the whole domestic staff. Extra waiters and kitchen help are called in to assist at large parties and state dinners.

The First Lady and her Social Secretary personally oversee all entertaining in the White House. Determining guest lists is always a major task. The Social Secretary helps to see that all the proper people are invited. A calligrapher uses special pens and styles of handwriting to address White House invitations. Three thousand or more invitations may be mailed out for a single event!

The Social Secretary also helps to see that everything runs smoothly and that the rules of etiquette and protocol are observed. At official dinners, the dinner partner and the placement of each guest depend upon his or her rank in the government or in the diplomatic corps. High-ranking guests sit near the President and his wife or official hostess. Letitia Baldrige was one of the most brilliant social secretaries to serve in the White House. She helped to make the Kennedy years such a special time.

The White House Kitchen

Franklin and Eleanor Roosevelt liked simple food. At Hyde Park, their family home on the Hudson River in New York, they served hot dogs—as typical American fare—to King George VI and Queen Elizabeth of Great Britain. But when they moved to the White House, they were shocked by the primitive state of the kitchen with its rotten floors and wooden iceboxes. They had the first modern kitchen installed with the latest refrigerator and freezer units and other modern appliances.

Several times in the last half-century, the White House kitchens have been completely modernized. But for the first fifty years after it was built, the cooks used two huge fireplaces in the big brick basement kitchen. In 1850, Millard Fillmore had an enormous black cast iron stove installed, but the cooks refused to use it until the President himself learned how it worked and then taught the others how to use it.

Hospitality and entertainment have always been an important part of life at the White House. A large cooking staff and a well-equipped kitchen have always been required. Cooks have had to keep abreast of the latest recipes and the most modern techniques. An 1887 cookbook used in the White House kitchen contains a recipe for potato chips. The crispy delicacy had just been invented in the horse-racing capital of nineteenth-century America, Saratoga, New York.

The Hoovers were among the most cultivated of all presidential couples and were also known for their gracious entertaining. Mrs. Hoover is thought by many to have set the best table in White House history. The Hoovers almost never ate a meal without a number of visitors and their simplest dinners had seven courses. Mrs. Hoover could deal successfully and easily with several thousand people at a time. Perfectly poised and meticulously organized, she was able to serve as hostess at two afternoon teas in separate rooms at the same time!

Today, it is not unusual for five thousand people to attend a White House reception, or for two hundred sitdown guests to be present at a state dinner. To handle this staggering entertainment load, the White House has kitchen facilities equal to those of a large restaurant or hotel. These include pantries, walk-in freezers, wine cellars, and portable ovens. Herb gardens supply some of the kitchen's needs, but in general everything must be bought—and in vast quantities.

Entertaining

Great receptions are held annually for members of Congress and for the judicial branch of the Government. In addition, special receptions are held for high-ranking officials of the armed forces.

Christmas is marked by a series of parties and receptions. Parties are always given for children of the White House staff and for the disadvantaged. One highlight of the national observance of Christmas in Washington is the President's lighting of the national Christmas tree set up in the Ellipse.

When George and Martha Washington resided in Philadelphia, they started the tradition of great New Year's Day receptions. When the Adamses moved into the White House, they brought this custom with them. The doors were thrown open to the public. By the nineteenth century, however, these receptions got out of hand. Visitors tracked up carpeting with dirty shoes and ruined valuable furnishings. They hacked off pieces of rugs and upholstery as souvenirs. But the tradition

*Each year the national Christmas tree
is set up on the Ellipse, near the White House.
The Washington Monument is in the background.*

was maintained until President Hoover abandoned the New Year's Day open house because it put such a great strain on the First Family—and on the White House itself!

Next to the burning by the British in 1814, the inaugural party of President Andrew Jackson in 1829 was one of the greatest scenes of devastation the White House has ever witnessed. After Jackson took the oath of office at the Capitol building, an uncontrollable mob descended upon the White House. Rowdy men in muddy boots clambered over elegant furniture to grab at food and drink. Hundreds of glasses and pieces of fine china, as well as a few noses, were broken in the brawls that ensued. It is surprising that no one was killed in the violent crush. Within hours, the crowd had reduced to rubble all the carefully prepared refreshments. To avoid being mauled, President Jackson escaped by a back exit and spent his first night in office at a local hotel.

Private Lives of the First Families

Home and family life are important to the American people and protecting the President's privacy and relaxation time is a high priority. Members of the Presidents' families spend a great deal of time avoiding cameras and newspeople. First Families have generally allowed few interviewers and photographers into their private quarters.

The President and the members of his family are public figures who enjoy little privacy. The White House Police Force constantly patrols the house and grounds. Secret Service agents serve as private bodyguards who follow the family everywhere to protect them from harm. They follow the President's children to school and accompany the First Lady when she makes public appearances. They even accompanied the Johnson girls and Susan Ford on dates! Plucky Eleanor Roosevelt, however, asserted her independence and refused to be followed by Secret Service agents. She drove her own car and often carried a pistol with her for protection!

Jacqueline Kennedy usually shunned photographers who pestered her whenever she appeared in public. But even earlier White House inhabitants longed for escape from the public eye. President Wilson's spirited daughters Margaret and Eleanor covered their faces with veils one afternoon and joined a sightseeing bus tour that passed the White House gate. No one recognized them, even when they begged the tour guide to let them go inside and meet the President's daughters.

To guard the President and his family, all gift parcels sent to the White House are X-rayed and examined for bombs or other dangerous substances by the mailroom staff. Almost everything that is sent unsolicited to the White House is turned over to charitable uses in Washington hospitals, nursing homes, and orphanages. Incoming telephone calls are carefully screened at a switchboard, although several years ago a young girl dialing numbers at random actually got her call through to the President's office!

Births and Weddings
at the White House

In 1806, Thomas Jefferson's married daughter, Martha Jefferson Randolph—who with her sister sometimes served as First Lady for their widowed father—gave birth to James Madison Randolph, the first baby to be born in the White House. Later, Grover Cleveland's wife Frances gave birth to Esther Cleveland, the only President's child to be born in the White House. The delivery room was a bedroom in the family living quarters on the second floor.

In addition to births, the White House has seen eighteen

official weddings of members of First Families. Dolley Madison planned the first White House wedding for her widowed sister, Lucy Payne Washington, to a Supreme Court justice in 1812. The only wedding of a President's son in the White House took place in 1828, when John Adams, son of John Quincy Adams and a grandson of John Adams, married his cousin Mary Catherine Hellen. In the days when the public could wander freely in and out, it is believed that many couples brought a Bible and a clergyman to perform a brief wedding service within the White House walls.

Grover Cleveland was a bachelor President until he married Frances Folsom in the Blue Room in 1886. The two other Presidents to be married during their presidential terms, Tyler and Wilson, were widowers who arranged their wedding ceremonies elsewhere.

Frances Cleveland became an enthusiastic First Lady. In 1889, on saying farewell to the White House staff after Cleveland had lost the 1888 election, she told them, "Take good care of all the furniture and ornaments—we are coming back!" Four years later they did come back, as President Cleveland began his second term of office, the only split term in American history.

Public Joy and Private Tragedy

More than one hundred and eighty children have lived in the White House, including children and grandchildren of Presidents, and those of other relatives living there. They have helped make the White House a lively place and a living place. In spite of the glamor of life in the public eye, the lives of several of our Presidents and First Ladies have been overshadowed by personal tragedies, including the loss of children. In some cases, this occurred before the families ever came to the White House, but the sad events still cast a pall of gloom over

President Grover Cleveland married Frances Folsom in the Blue Room. To date, this is the only wedding of a President to take place in the White House.

life there. Two of the sons of President Franklin Pierce had died in childhood. A third son was killed by a railroad train two months before Pierce's inauguration.

During the Civil War, Abraham Lincoln's son Willie died of a fever, adding to Lincoln's grief over the war-torn country. But another Lincoln son, Tad, went on amusing the American public with his antics. President McKinley's invalid wife Ida continued to mourn for her two daughters who had died several years before the McKinleys came to the White House.

In 1924, the Coolidges lost their son Calvin, Jr. to blood poisoning from an infected blister he got playing tennis on the White House Courts. And months before his assassination, John F. Kennedy and his wife Jacqueline lost their newborn son Patrick to a congenital respiratory ailment.

Animals at the White House

Among the other memorable inhabitants of the White House and its grounds have been the exotic assortment of pets and other animals. Thomas Jefferson kept a pair of grizzly bears on the White House lawn that had been sent to him from the West by the Lewis and Clark Expedition. President Benjamin Harrison's son kept a pet goat, His Whiskers. The children of Theodore Roosevelt once rode up and down the White House elevator with a pony!

The Tafts were the last presidential family to keep farm animals at the White House—a flock of chickens and a milk cow named Pauline Wayne. During World War I, President Wilson kept a flock of sheep on the lawn to trim the grass, since this would release additional men for military service! President Harding tried to breed turkeys in a pen on the lawn. The Kennedys kept a whole menagerie of pets—including Caroline's pony Macaroni—even though President Kennedy was allergic to them. And many people remember President Lyndon B. Johnson lifting his beagles, Him and Her, by their ears.

CONCLUSION

No home of a world leader is so involved in the history and fortune of its country as is the White House. And the families who live there seem to lead charmed and privileged existences. Sometimes, there is even a tendency to think of them as royalty. But the President of the United States is elected for a term that lasts only four years. And every four or eight years, an entirely new family moves into the White House to make it their home for a brief time. Always the White House remains a representative American home, the essence of American family values and life-styles. The White House and its contents show that it has always been in the vanguard of American housing, with the latest achievements of science, invention, fashion, and taste.

    Although Presidents have made additions and alterations, the White House retains its basic original plan and appearance. Its rooms still hold many mementos of the home's historic occupants. Fortunately, in addition to the White House memorabilia, there is a wealth of other material relating to the Presidents. Many members of First Families kept diaries and journals which have been preserved, and, in the days before the telephone, almost all were great letter writers.

    Presidential papers of all kinds have been left in public archives in Washington and in presidential libraries that have been built in many parts of the country. As public figures, the Presidents were the subjects of numerous newspaper and mag-

President-elect and Mrs. Ronald Reagan are greeted at the diplomatic entrance of the White House by President and Mrs. Carter shortly after the 1980 election.

azine accounts and books during their terms of office. Scholars and historians continue to study the lives of the Presidents, looking for clues that can shed new light on the inhabitants of the White House, their personalities, and their times.

Many of our Presidents and First Ladies have been people who first visited the White House as children or young adults. And perhaps some of the young men and women who read and learn about the White House today will later come to live or work there.

FOR FURTHER READING

Aikman, Lonnelle. *The Living White House.* Washington, D.C.: White House Historical Association, revised edition, 1978.

Blumberg, Rhoda. *First Ladies* (A First Book). New York: Franklin Watts, 1977.

Bourne, Miriam A. *White House Children.* New York: Random House, 1979.

Reit, Seymour. *Growing up in the White House: The Story of the President's Children.* New York; Macmillan, 1968.

Seuling, Barbara. *The Last Cow on the White House Lawn and Other Little Known Facts About the Presidency.* New York: Doubleday, 1977.

White House Historical Association. *The White House: An Historic Guide.* Washington, D.C.: 1962.

INDEX

Adams, Abigail, 6–7, 28, 39, 42, 43, 49
Adams, John, 1, 6–7, 33, 39, 43, 49, 53
Animals in White House, 55–56
Apartments, presidential, 44–45
Architects, 4–5, 6, 9, 10, 14, 31
Army Corps of Engineers, 10
Arthur, Chester Alan, 12
Attic, 13, 21, 37

Bathroom, first, 43
Births in White House, 52
Blair House, 17, 24
Blue Room, 27, 30, 31, 32, 34, 54
Bomb shelter, 17, 25
British soldiers, 7, 8, 30, 51
Broadcasting room, 17
Buchanan, James, 12
Building of White House, 6
Burning of White House, 7, 8, 30, 51

Cabinet Room, 24, 36
Capitol, 1, 4–5, 33, 51
Carter, Amy, 36
Carter, President Jimmy, 2, 23
Carter, Rosalynn, 19
Children in White House, 11, 46, 53, 55
China collection, 10
China Room, 26
Christmas tree, 49, 50
Cleveland, Grover, 52, 53, 54
Committee for the Preservation of the White House, 19
Coolidge, Calvin, 13, 55
Cornerstone, laying of, 6

Cost of reconstruction, 14, 17
Cost of White House, 5

Decorations, 12, 30, 32
Diplomatic Reception Room, 25, 26, 31
Downing, Andrew Jackson, 39

East End, 13
Easter Egg Roll, 40
East Room, 7, 27, 28, 29, 30, 37, 42
East Terrace, 25, 26
East Wing, 13, 24–25, 26, 27, 41
Eisenhower, President, 40
Electricity, first, 44
Elevators, 44
Ellipse, 42, 49, 50
Emancipation Proclamation, signing of, 2, 37
Entertaining, 29, 30, 31, 33, 37, 39, 40, 47, 48, 49, 51
Entrance Hall, 27, 34
Entrances, 19, 25, 31
Executive Office Building, new, 24
Executive Protective Service, 24

Family Dining Room, 34
Fine Arts Committee, 18
"Fireside chats," 3, 26
Fires, White House, 7, 8, 13, 30, 51
First Families' private lives, 51–52
First Ladies, 44–45, 47
First Lady's offices, 13, 24–25
Ford, Betty, 19
Ford, President Gerald R., 35
Ford, Susan, 51
Franklin, Benjamin, 31

[60]

Furnishings, 2, 9, 12, 18, 27, 30, 31, 32, 48

Garden, children's, 39
Garden Room, 25
Grant, President, 11, 12, 39
Greenhouses, 12, 13, 19, 46
Green Room, 27, 30–31
Ground Floor, 26–34
Grounds, 39–40, 41

Harding, Warren, 44, 55
Harrison, Benjamin, 44, 55
Harrison, Mrs. Benjamin, 10
Harrison, William Henry, 42
Hayes, Lucy, 40, 45, 46
Hayes, Rutherford B., 33, 40, 44
Heating system, first, 43
Hoban, James, 5, 9, 31, 33
Hoover, President and Mrs., 48–49, 51
Housekeeping staff, 47–48, 49

Improvements in White House, 43–44, 48

Jackson, Andrew, *frontis*, 19, 40, 51
Jefferson, Thomas, 6, 24, 31, 33, 42, 43, 45, 52, 55
Johnson, Lady Bird, 2, 19
Johnson, Lyndon B., 2, 38, 39, 56

Kennedy, Caroline, 39, 55
Kennedy, John F., 2, 55
Kennedy, Mrs. John F., 19–20, 25, 26, 27, 28, 30, 52, 55
Kitchen, 48

Latrobe, Benjamin, 6, 9
L'Enfant, Major Pierre, 4–5
Library, 26

Life at the White House, 42–56
Lincoln Bedroom, 18, 36, 37, 38
Lincoln, President, 2, 28, 35, 37, 55
Lincoln Sitting Room, 37

Madison, Dolley, 7, 33, 40, 47, 53
Madison, James, 7, 40
Maintenance of White House, 10, 18–19, 27
Marriages in White House, 28, 40, 52–53, 54
McKinley, William, 10, 55
Monroe, James, 9, 30, 31, 34

National Park Service, 10
New White House, plans for, 9
Nixon, Pat, 19, 30, 40
Nixon, Richard M., 2, 40
North Entrance, 25
North Portico, 9, 19, 25, 36, 39

Occupants of White House, first, 6
Offices, presidential, 13, 21, 22, 24, 36, 41
Old Executive Office Building, 24
Oval Office, 22

Pennsylvania Avenue, 5, 17, 19, 22, 24, 36, 39
Physician's office, 27
Police Force, 51
Polk, James, 33, 43
Portraits of First Ladies, 26
Portraits of Presidents, 2, 7, 34, 35
Protocol, 47–48

Queens' Bedroom, 37

Radio, first, 44
Rebuilding White House, 9, 15–16, 39, 44

Reconstruction of White House, 14–17
Red Room, 27, 30, 33
Roosevelt, Eleanor, 48, 51–52
Roosevelt, Franklin D., 2, 3, 7, 13, 22, 26, 28, 48
Roosevelt, Theodore, 9, 12, 25, 34, 36, 55
Rose Garden, 22, 23, 24, 40

Second Floor, 36–37
Secret Service, 24, 51, 52
Servants' quarters, 6
Social Secretary, 47
Solarium, 39
South Entrance, 25
South Portico, 9, 13, 14, 21, 31, 39
Staff, presidential, 24, 42, 47–48, 49
State Dining Room, 7, 13, 27, 33–34, 35, 36
State rooms, 27–34
Stuart, Gilbert, 7
Swimming pools, 13, 22, 45

Taft, William Howard, 43, 44, 45
Telephone, first, 44

Tennis courts, 39, 55
Third floor and roof, 39
Tragedy in the White House, 53, 55
Treaty Room, 36
Truman balcony, 17
Truman, Harry S., 13, 14, 37, 44
Tunnel to Treasury Building, 25

Van Burens, 31, 47
Vermeil Room, 26
Visiting hours, 27, 40

Washington, building city of, 4–5
Washington, George, 1, 4–6, 7, 24, 49
Washington, Martha, 4, 6, 49
West Terrace, 12, 13, 22
West Wing, 13, 21, 22, 24, 36, 39, 41
White House, first use of name, 9
White House Historical Association, 18, 19
Wilson, Edith, 45

Yellow Drawing Room, 33
Yellow Oval Room, 31, 36

ABOUT THE AUTHOR

Cass R. Sandak is a writer who divides his time between Manhattan and upstate New York. He has worked in publishing and public relations, including assignments with Letitia Baldrige. In his free moments, he enjoys traveling and is active in community affairs.

Mr. Sandak is the author of five Easy-Read Holiday Books, *Christmas, Easter, Halloween, Thanksgiving,* and *Valentine's Day,* also published by Franklin Watts.